i love crochet

i love crochet

25 PROJECTS THAT WILL SHOW YOU HOW TO CROCHET EASILY AND QUICKLY

RACHEL HENDERSON & SARAH HAZELL

PHOTOGRAPHY BY KATE WHITAKER

RODALE®

First published in Great Britain in 2007 by
Kyle Cathie Limited, 122 Arlington Road, London NW1 7HP, United Kingdom
general.enquiries@kylecathie.com
www.kylecathie.com

First published in 2008 by Rodale Inc.

Rodale books may be purchased for business or promotional use or for special sales. For information, please write to: Special Markets Department, Rodale, Inc., 733 Third Avenue, New York, NY 10017

Internet addresses and telephone numbers given in this book were accurate at the time it went to press.

Photographs by Kate Whitaker
Illustrations by Roberta Boyce
Book design by Kyle Cathie Limited
Printed in Singapore

Library of Congress Cataloging-in-Publication Data
Henderson, Rachel.
   I love crochet : 25 projects that will show you how to crochet easily and quickly / Rachel Henderson & Sarah Hazell.
     p.   cm.
   Includes index.
   ISBN-13 978–1–60529–942–6 paperback
   ISBN-10 1–60529–942–1 paperback
   1. Crocheting–Patterns. I. Hazell, Sarah. II. Title.
TT820.H53 2008
746.43'4041—dc22   2008015464

Distributed to the book trade by Macmillan
2 4 6 8 10 9 7 5 3 1 paperback

We inspire and enable people to improve their lives and the world around them
For more of our products visit rodalestore.com or call 800-848-4735

acknowledgments

We have loved every minute of working on this book. It has been a journey in our world of crafts we will never forget and we would like to say a big thank you to everyone at Kyle Cathie who gave us the chance to work on such a fun project. Our editors, Danielle and Muna, our copyeditor, Karen, photographer Kate, illustrator Roberta, designer Jenny and all our gorgeous models!

I would really like to say a big thank you to Sharon Brant for all her help and encouragement since starting out at Rowan Yarns, and Rein Hilde Van Der Brand for teaching me some of those very cool crochet techniques! Most of all I would like to thank Sarah for her constant enthusiasm, inspiration and humor while working on the book and not forgetting my parents for continuing to support me throughout my knitting and crocheting journey.

Rachel x

My first thank you must go to Rachel for inviting me to join her in writing the book—totally cool! A huge thank you to Sharon Brant at Rowan Yarns who got me crocheting in the first place and who never fails to support me and make me laugh! Also to the many fabulous knitters and designers I have met through Rowan—Emma King, Debbie Abrahams, Jane Crowfoot: they never fail to inspire and encourage. A special thank you to Shubhen Chitnis up in Holmfirth for keeping me supplied with yarn. My ability to write the book would not have been possible without the help of friends—Alison, Karen, Vic and Julie; and my amazing family —Simon, mum and dad—the best! My fantastic husband, Paul, and wonderful daughter, Phoebe—so many thanks and even more love!
Dedicated to the memory of my beautiful dog, Merton.

Sarah

contents

our crochet story

As committed (ok, obsessive) knitters it took quite a lot of time for us even to pick up a crochet hook. In fact, the thought of using just a single hook seemed almost impossible and certainly asymmetrical. Nonetheless, curiosity finally won over, and once we'd worked out how to hold the yarn and hook correctly, we discovered how wrong we'd been.

We are now mad crocheters. Like knitting, the possibilities are endless and the designs fantastic. You can work not only in two, but three dimensions. You don't have to stick to yarn; why not use some wire, string, or even leather? Crochet is also fast, flexible, and completely forgiving if you make the odd mistake. In fact, it's becoming quite a craze, with cutting-edge designs routinely popping up on the runways of the world, and more and more people reaching for their hook and yarn. Most people are surprised when we say it can be an easier craft to master than knitting, with less terminology and less jargon, leading to less time for confusion and more time to create some fabulous designs!

what you can make

Our projects range from funky, original items you can wear, like a stripey scarf or a hat and glove combo, to some elegant evening purses and jewelry pieces. In the Crocheting For An Occasion chapter, you can create your own place mats and coasters, bottle bags and rag rugs. We'll even show you some great ideas for original artwork—perfect for gifts. Once you've awakened the designer in you, you can move onto some of our customizing ideas. These are fantastic ways of breathing new life into your old clothes, as well as adding your own personal touches to some affordable high street basics.

crochet for life

By far the best part of crochet is that it's completely mobile. Standing in line, commuting, and even sitting around chatting with friends can be brightened up with a hook and yarn. Your first project could be a great yarn bag—perfect for carting your stuff about with you at all times.

We have loved working on this book, inspiring each other throughout, and hopefully inspiring you too. Most of all we want you to have fun with our designs and make them your own.

Rachel x Sarah

how to crochet

We'll begin this section by saying, don't worry, the key to crochet is persistence, so don't get disheartened after a few attempts. Once you've got a grasp of the basics, it's all about practicing how to hold the yarn and perfecting how to move the hook so that you can achieve a good gauge. As your confidence starts to grow you can start adding beads and sequins or move onto our decorative stitches. Most of all, have fun and think creatively. Good luck!

choosing a hook & yarn

Holding a crochet hook and yarn is very straightforward. In fact, it really shouldn't take long before it becomes second nature. It's so easy, you'll soon be crocheting on the bus or when you're hanging out with your friends.

Pure merino super-chunky wool

Multicolored bulky wool

Lambswool, kid mohair, and nylon mixed heavy weight yarn

YARNS

There are many different types of yarns on the market. Each type of yarn has a particular weight and composition. Depending on the size of hook you use, they all give a different type of fabric. Crochet makes a thicker and firmer fabric than knitting, so take that into account when choosing your yarn, hook, and stitch.

The three factors you should consider when choosing a yarn are its weight (or thickness), composition (what it's made of) and length.

Weight This is based on the number of plies (or strands) the yarn is made of. The thinnest yarn is superfine and it goes up in size through light, medium, heavy and bulky to extra-bulky.

Composition Yarns are made up of different fibers, from natural ones such as merino wool, alpaca, silk, cotton, and linen to man-made ones like nylon, acrylic, and viscose. The yarn's label will tell you what the yarn is made of and give you washing information.

Length The yardage of yarn in a ball can vary, even if the yarns are the same type and the balls weigh the same. It is the yardage that is vital, so check the ball for the yardage and make sure you buy enough for the total length required by the pattern.

HOOKS

Crochet hooks come in different types, shapes, and sizes. It's up to you to decide whether you prefer hooks made of aluminum, steel, plastic, or bamboo. Steel and aluminum hooks often have a strong plastic middle and end, which is easy to grip and lighter on your fingers. Some hooks have a flat middle, which is also easy to grip. Try out different hooks until you find the one that's most comfortable for you.

The size of hook you use is all-important. A pattern will always recommend which size to use, but it depends on the weight of the yarn and your gauge. If you use a big hook with bulky yarn, your crochet will grow quickly, or more slowly if you opt for a smaller hook. Crochet hooks are generally the same length as you only ever have a few loops on the hook at any given time.

If you choose a different yarn from the one suggested, it's important to match the gauge to the one given in the pattern. For more information on gauge, see page 14.

Softly twisted bulky cotton and acrylic mix

Pure silk medium yarn

Medium wool and cotton mix

Super kid mohair and silk mixed light

equipment

All you really need is some yarn and a hook that's comfortable to use. But, as you make more projects, you might like to buy a few more pieces of equipment that will make your life a little easier.

1 Ruler or tape measure This is a handy thing to have, especially when checking your gauge square at the beginning of a project.

2 Sewing needles A tapestry needle is used for darning ends and sewing your crocheted project. If you are using a very bulky yarn, make sure you choose a needle with an eye large enough to take the yarn. You may also need a finer needle if you wish to incorporate beads in your crochet.

3 Scissors A small pair of scissors is always useful for trimming ends of yarn.

4 Pins When you are sewing your crocheted project, you will find these helpful for keeping the fabric in place.

5 Notepad and pen Always useful to have on hand, especially if you are designing a new project, or just need to keep count of your rows, rounds, and different stitches.

6 Crochet stitch markers These help to identify which row you are on—especially handy when you are working in a round.

gauge

The way you hold the yarn and hook will give you a specific gauge determining how tight or loose your crocheted fabric is.

Gauge is how tightly or loosely you crochet—or the number of stitches and rows in a given crocheted fabric. The gauge will affect the size of your finished project. If you crochet more tightly than the pattern recommends, your project will end up too small, and if you crochet more loosely, it might be too big.

Always crochet a gauge square before you start a project. Use the same yarn, type of stitch, and size of hook as the pattern recommends, and check that your gauge matches the pattern.

If you want to use a different yarn, it must also give the same gauge. Use the same stitch because each one gives a different height, which will affect the

number of rows in a given measurement. If you want to change the type of stitch suggested in a pattern, you will need to calculate how many more or fewer rows make the same length of fabric. The thickness of a crochet hook of the same size can vary slightly, which might affect your gauge—so you may need to change to a bigger or a smaller size to get the right gauge.

MEASURING YOUR GAUGE SQUARE

The pattern will tell you how many stitches and rows you should have in a 4 inches square. Crochet a slightly larger square and fasten it off. Place a tape measure horizontally across the square and, starting a few stitches from the edge, position pins 4 inches apart. Count the stitches between the pins.

Then place the tape measure vertically across the square and position pins 4 inches apart. Count the number of rows between the pins.

When working a more decorative stitch pattern, your gauge will be measured according to the repeat pattern rather than the number of stitches and rows. In that case, count the number of pattern repeats between the pins.

If you have too few stitches or repeats, try again with a larger hook. If you have too many, use a smaller hook. Don't try to crochet at a different gauge to what comes naturally—you won't be able to keep it up throughout the project.

holding your hook & yarn

Holding your crochet hook and yarn can feel awkward at first. But persistence is the key and once it feels right, you're off! Try holding the hook loosely just before you start to work with the yarn, either with an overhand grip or as if you were holding a pen.

HOLDING THE HOOK

Here are the two most common ways of holding the hook in your right hand. Practice both and find the way that feels most comfortable.

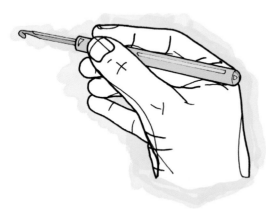

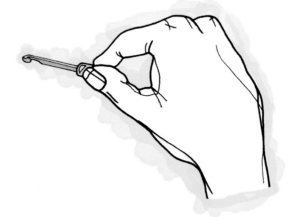

Writing grip Hold the middle of the hook between your thumb and index finger, so that the hooked side is facing you and the rest of it is supported by your hand—just as if you are about to write with it.

Overhand grip Hold the middle of the hook with the tips of your thumb and index finger, so that the hooked side is facing you and your hand is above the hook.

HOLDING THE YARN

With the hook in your right hand, you'll need your left hand to hold your work and the yarn. It's worth getting this right, as the way you hold the yarn controls the gauge and keeps it even. Practice both methods to see which way works best for you.

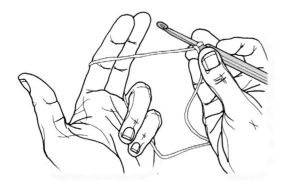

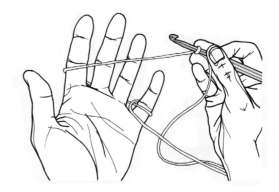

Two-finger grip Wrap the working end of the yarn (the one attached to the ball) loosely around the back of the index and middle fingers on your left hand. Grip the yarn firmly with your last two fingers against your hand.

One-finger grip Wrap the working end of the yarn around the back of the first three fingers on your left hand. Bring it in front of your little finger and wrap it right around that finger again. You can tighten your grip on the yarn by pressing your little finger against your ring finger.

HOLDING THE WORK

With the working end of the yarn secure, take tight hold of your work with your left thumb and index finger close to the hook. Don't hold the hook too tight or your gauge will be tight.

basic techniques

To start any crochet you need a foundation chain. It's just like a cast-on row in knitting and provides the basic foundation for the rest of the crocheted fabric. The number of chains you make determines the width of the fabric.

SLIP KNOT

1 To start a foundation chain, leave a short tail of yarn and make a slip knot by winding the yarn twice around two fingers on your left hand. Hold the loose end of yarn secure with your thumb and take the second loop behind the first one.

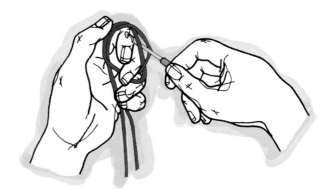

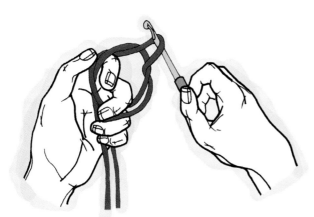

2 Pull the second loop of yarn through the first loop either with the crochet hook or your right-hand fingers.

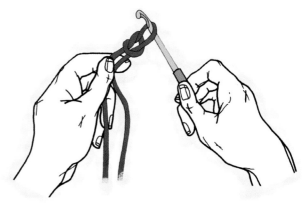

3 Slip the new loop onto the crochet hook and tighten it up by gently pulling on the loose end of yarn. Remember not to make the slip knot too tight; you can slacken it off again by gently pulling on the working end of the yarn.

MAKING A FOUNDATION CHAIN

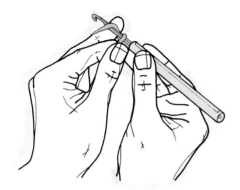

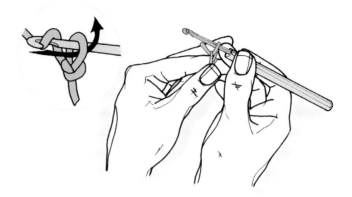

1 Firmly hold the slip knot with your left index finger and thumb. Hold the crochet hook in your right hand. Lifting your left middle finger to tighten the yarn, slide the hook over the working yarn from above (this often called "yarn over" or "yo"). Rotating the hook slightly, secure the yarn under the hook end.

2 Pull the hook back through the slip knot. Repeat this process, continually adjusting your left-hand grip to hold the work near the hook, until the required number of chain stitches has been made.

RACHEL'S & SARAH'S TIP:
When making your foundation chain, make sure the chain stitches aren't too tight, otherwise it can be difficult to get the hook through each chain stitch for your next row.

COUNTING CHAIN STITCHES

Count your chains before you begin the next row, then you'll be sure to make the right width of fabric.

Make sure the foundation chain is not twisted and that the fronts of the chains are facing you. Count the number of loops—each one counts as one chain stitch. When you count, always ignore the initial slip knot and the loop on your hook.

WORKING INTO THE FOUNDATION CHAIN

With the right length of foundation chain, you are ready to work the first row. This can be quite tricky if the foundation chain is tight and it can be hard to see each chain stitch. Here are two ways of working—either will make it easier.

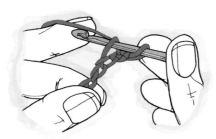

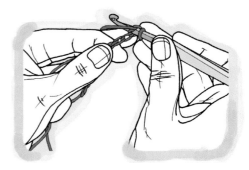

Method 1 Flip the foundation chain over and slide the crochet hook from front to back through the top of the second chain stitch from the hook. Take the working yarn over the hook. Draw the yarn through the foundation chain stitch to make another loop on the hook. Complete the new chain stitch according to the pattern. Make the next stitch into the very next chain on the foundation chain. Continue in this way to the end.

Method 2 If you hold the foundation chain with the fronts of the chain stitches facing you, you can see that they each make a sideways "v" shape. Slide the hook from front to back under the second "v" shape from the hook, making sure it goes under two loops. Take the working yarn over the hook and draw it through so there's a loop on the hook. Complete the new stitch according to the pattern. Make the next stitch into the very next "v" shape on the foundation chain. Continue to the end.

MAKING A TURNING CHAIN

To keep the shape of your crochet even, you need to make one or more turning chains at the beginning of each row. These are simple chain stitches and the number you need depends on the type of stitch in the next row. The number of stitches you need in your turning chain to match various stitches are given are as follows:

Single crochet: 1 turning chain
Half double crochet: 2 turning chains
Double crochet: 3 turning chains
Treble crochet: 4 turning chains

When you work most stitches, count the turning chain as the first stitch. However, when you are working single crochet, ignore the turning chain—it doesn't count as a stitch.

basic stitches

Here are a few stitches you can work into the foundation chain. They are all worked in the same basic way, but the differences are achieved by changing the number of times you wind the yarn around the hook and the number of loops you pull the hook through.

SLIP STITCH (ss)

This is used to sew crocheted fabrics and to complete a round.

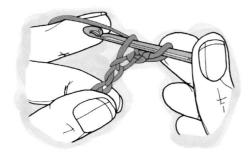

1 Slide the hook through the last chain stitch worked on the foundation chain to give two loops on the hook. Take the working yarn over the hook.

2 Draw the hook, and yarn, back through both loops on the hook. Slide the hook through the next chain stitch on the foundation chain and repeat the process to the end of the row.

WORKING IN ROWS

Always work from right to left along the rows. When you come to the end of a row you will need to turn your work. It doesn't matter whether you turn it clockwise or counter-clockwise—as long as you turn it the same way every time, the fabric will stay flat.

Your yarn should always be sitting at the back of your work before you make your chain stitches at the beginning of a new row. This will enable you to maintain a straight and neat edge.

SINGLE CROCHET (sc)

This is one of the simplest, and most commonly used, crochet stitches.

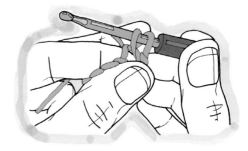

1 At the beginning of the row, first add one extra chain stitch to make the turning chain. Then slide the hook into the second chain stitch on the foundation chain.

2 Take the working yarn over the hook and pull the yarn back through the first loop on the hook. Take the yarn over again and pull it back through both loops to give just one new loop on the hook. Repeat steps 1 to 2 to the end of the row, working into the next chain stitch on the foundation chain.

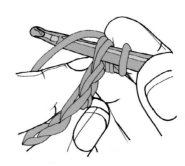

3 At the end of the row, turn your work and make one turning chain. On all rows after the first one, make single crochets in the same way as in steps 1 and 2, but sliding the hook under both loops at the top of each stitch (the "v" shape described on page 20).

DOUBLE CROCHET (dc)

Double crochet produces an open fabric because the yarn is wound around the hook three times to create long stitches.

1 At the beginning of the row, first add a turning chain of three extra stitches. Take the working yarn over the hook. Then slide the hook into the fourth chain from the hook on the foundation chain.

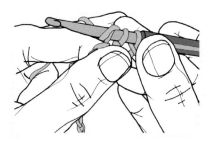

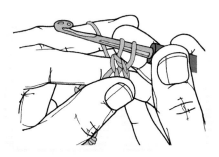

2 Take the yarn over the hook and pull it back through the first loop on the hook. You should now have three loops on the hook again.

3 Take the yarn over the hook and pull it back through the first two loops on the hook. You will now have two loops on the hook. ➤

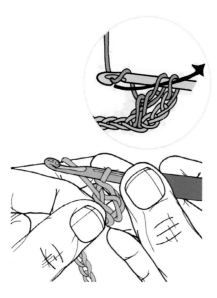

④ Take the yarn over the hook again and pull it back through the last two loops to give one new loop on the hook. Repeat steps 1 to 4 to the end of the row, working into each chain stitch on the foundation chain.

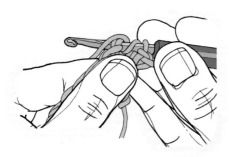

⑤ At the end of the row, turn your work and make three turning chains. On all rows after the first one, make double crochets into the doubles on the previous row in the same way as in steps 1 to 4, but missing the first double and sliding the hook under both loops at the top of each stitch (the "v" shape described on page 20). At the end of the row, work the last double into the top of the turning chain.

HALF DOUBLE (hdc)

The name of this stitch describes it well—it's a slightly shorter version of the double.

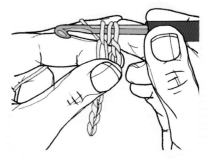

① At the beginning of the row, first add a turning chain of two extra chain stitches. Take the working yarn over the hook. Then slide the hook into the third chain stitch on the foundation chain. Pull the yarn back through the first loop on the hook. You should now have three loops on your needle.

TREBLE (tr)

This is a slightly taller stitch than the double and gives you a very open fabric.

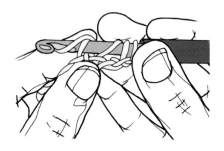

2 Take the yarn over the hook again and pull the yarn through all three loops to give one new loop on the hook. Repeat steps 1 to 2 to the end of the row, working into each next chain stitch on the foundation chain.

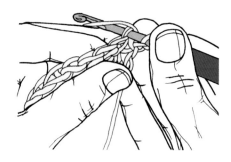

1 At the beginning of the row, first add a turning chain of four extra stitches. Take the working yarn over the hook, twice. Then slide the hook into the fifth chain from the hook on the foundation chain. Take the yarn over the hook again, just once. ➤

3 At the end of the row, turn your work and make two turning chains. On all rows after the first one, make half double crochets into the half doubles on the previous row in the same way as in steps 1 to 2, but missing the first half double and sliding the hook under both loops at the top of each stitch (the "v" shaped described on page 20). At the end of the row, work the last half double into the top of the turning chain.

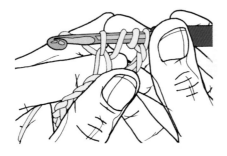

2 Pull the crochet hook through the first loop on the hook. You will now have four loops on the hook.

3 Now take the yarn over the hook again and pull it back through the first two loops on the hook. You will now have three loops left on the hook.

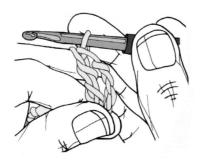

4 Repeat step 3, pulling the yarn through the next two loops on the hook. Repeat again and pull the

yarn through the last two loops to give one remaining loop. Repeat steps 1 to 4 to the end of the row, working into each next chain stitch on the foundation row.

5 At the end of the row, turn your work and make four turning chains. On all rows after the first one, make treble crochets into the double trebles on the previous row in the same way as in steps 1 to 4, but missing the first treble and sliding the hook under both loops at the top of each stitch (the "v" shape described on page 20). At the end of the row, work the last treble into the top of the turning chain.

next steps

Now that you can do the basic stitches, you're ready to learn some more techniques before you tackle a project.

JOINING IN NEW YARN

Always make sure you have enough yarn to crochet to the end of the row. But don't panic—if you run out, there's a way of joining new working yarn into your fabric.

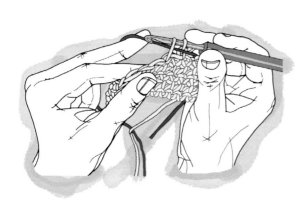

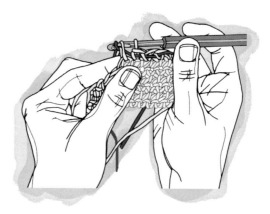

1 Start to work in the end of the new yarn a few stitches before you finish the old yarn. Do this by laying it along the top of the previous row so that you work over it as you make the next few stitches.

2 When you need to change yarns, draw the first loops for the next stitch through with the old yarn. Then pick up the new yarn and draw it through to make the last loop of the stitch. Continue with the new yarn, working over the end of the old yarn to secure it. Neatly snip off the two ends of yarn.

CHANGING COLOR

Working in different colors is so easy when you are crocheting. You can join in a new color in the middle or at the end of a row and when working in a round.

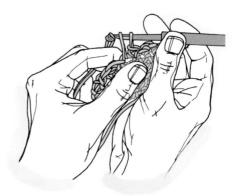

❶ Wherever you join in the new color, make the previous stitch with the old color, but without pulling through the final loop. Drop the old color and pick up the new one, and complete the stitch with the new color of yarn.

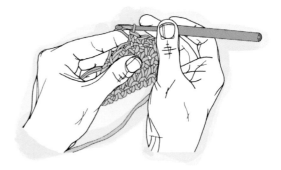

❷ Continue working with the new color of yarn. If you joined the yarns in the middle of a row or in a round, fasten off the yarns through stitches of the same color and neatly snip off the ends.

If you are working stripes of color, just leave the yarns that will be used later hanging at the ends of the rows. As you return to a hanging yarn, twist it once around the working yarn so that it gets carried up the side of the fabric. Start to use the hanging yarn again when it is required, dropping the old yarn for later use.

FASTENING OFF

When you've finished your crocheted fabric, you will need to fasten off.

Make one chain. Cut the yarn with about a 6in end. Then pull the end firmly through the chain to secure it. Either leave the end for sewing later or weave it in.

WEAVING IN ENDS

Ends of yarn need to be woven carefully into the crocheted fabric so that they can't be seen and won't unravel. It's often convenient to weave them into a seam, or failing that, through the backs of stitches on the wrong side.

Thread the end into a tapestry needle and then weave it through the back of several crochet stitches. Don't pull the yarn tight or it will pucker the fabric. Carefully trim off the end.

WORKING IN ROUNDS

This is such a fun technique and really simple to do. Check out the hot-water bag cover on page 99, which would be a great project to use to start practicing your circles!

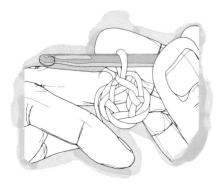

To begin working in rounds you still need to make a foundation chain, with the number of chains stated in the pattern. Then make a slip stitch (see page 21) through the first loop in the foundation chain to join the two ends of the chain together. This gives you a base ring for your design.

To begin all the following rounds, make a starting chain. It's just like a turning chain (see page 20) and needs to have the appropriate number of chains for the stitch you are going to use. For example, if you are going to work in single crochet, you will make just one chain. ➤

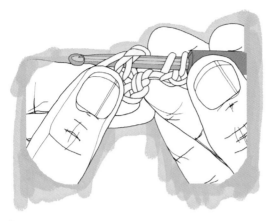

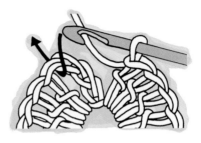

2 To work the stitches for the first round, always insert the hook through the middle of the base ring to draw through the first loop.

3 To finish the first round, insert the hook through the top of the starting chain and work a slip stitch.

RACHEL'S & SARAH'S TIP:
Use a crochet stitch marker to keep track of where you began each round. Every time you begin a round, place a colored marker on top of your starting chain. If you do not add a marker, it can be easy to confuse which round you are working on, and you may end up adding or losing stitches.

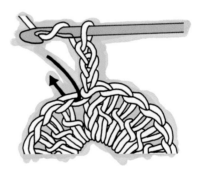

4 For the second round, make a starting chain as usual. Make the stitches on this and all following rounds by inserting the hook under both loops at the top of each stitch on the previous round. Complete the round with a slip stitch.

To keep your crocheted fabric flat, you will need to work two stitches into each stitch on the previous round, increasing (see also page 39) the total number of stitches in each round.

easy decorative stitches

Once you have mastered all the basic stitches, there are lots of ways of working them to create a variety of textures, patterns, and shapes. They will give your fabric interest as well as form the basis for making edgings, buttonholes, and fancy motifs.

This sample was worked in single crochet.

WORKING BETWEEN STITCHES

You can work in this way with any type of stitch to create a very firm fabric. The taller the stitch, the easier it will be to maneuver the hook.

Insert the hook between two stitches on the previous row, instead of under the top of a stitch. Finish the stitch in the usual way and repeat this way of working across the row.

Always count the stitches after you finish the row to check that you still have the correct number.

Three doubles were worked into each three chain spaces on both samples.

WORKING INTO CHAIN SPACES

If you work into the spaces made by chains along rows or in rounds, you can open up the spaces to create interesting patterns. You can use this method in lots of ways, including making buttonholes, motifs, and edgings.

Insert the hook underneath the whole chain on the previous row and then complete working the new stitch in the usual way. Work the number of stitches into one chain space as directed by the pattern.

2sc, 3dc, 2sc worked into each five chain spaces in this sample.

An attractive variation for an edging is to change the stitches worked into the chain space. For example, begin with single crochet, increasing to doubles in the middle and then returning to single crochet.

FRONT AND BACK LOOP CROCHET

Working into the front or the back of stitches produces slightly different effects, but both with distinctive horizontal bars across the fabric.

To work into the front of the loop, simply insert the hook upward under just the front loop of the stitch on the previous row. Complete the new stitch in the usual way.

To work into the back of the loop, simply insert the hook downward under just the back loop of the stitch on the previous row. Complete the new stitch in the usual way.

Try experimenting with both these techniques to create more interesting fabrics.

This sample was made by working into the front loops on every row.

This sample was made with alternating rows of front and back crochet.

CROSSED STITCHES

There are several ways of creating crossed stitches. You can cross pairs of short or tall stitches, but the taller the stitch, the clearer the crossed shape.

Make a foundation chain with an even number of chain stitches and then work a turning chain to suit your chosen stitch. Miss one stitch in the previous row and work the new stitch into the next stitch on the previous row. Then work the second new stitch into the missed stitch on the previous row. Repeat this pattern across the row.

This sample has been worked by crossing single double crochets.

fun textured variations

When you start designing your own crocheted accessories or garments there are many decorative effects you can create just using the basic stitches.

This sample was crocheted in
DK yarn with a 4.5mm hook.
See pattern below right.

popcorn stitch

Popcorns are groups of complete stitches worked into the same stitch and then closed together at the top to create a very textured fabric. They are often worked in double, and half double or treble crochet.

HOW TO MAKE A POPCORN

This method is for a three-stitch popcorn, but you can also make popcorns with more or fewer stitches.

Work three double stitches into the same stitch on the previous row. Remove the hook from the working loop and insert it under both loops at the top of the first double. Insert the hook back into the working loop and pull it through the other loops on the hook to close the popcorn.

TRY THIS POPCORN PATTERN

Foundation chain: ch a number of sts divisible by 3 plus 2.
Foundation row: 1ch, work in sc across row.
Row 1: 3ch, 1dc, * work popcorn, 2dc*.
Row 2: 1ch, sc across row.
Continue, repeating both these 2 rows.
Fasten off.

bobbles

Each bobble is a cluster of incomplete stitches worked into the same stitch. They are often worked in double crochet, with shorter stitches on each side to enhance the bumpy effect on the bobbles.

HOW TO MAKE BOBBLE (MB)

This method is for a five-stitch bobble, but you can also make bobbles with more or fewer stitches.

Work five double stitches into the same stitch on the previous row, but leave the last loop of each one on the hook. You should have six loops on the hook.

Take the yarn over the hook again and draw it through all six loops on the hook, ready to progress to the next stitch.

This sample was crocheted in
DK yarn with a 4.5mm hook.
See pattern below left.

TRY THIS BOBBLE PATTERN

Foundation chain: ch a number of sts divisible by 4 plus 3 extra.
Foundation row and first two rows: 1ch, work in sc across row.
Row 3: 3ch, 2dc, *MB, 3dc* rep across row.
Rows 4–6: 1ch, work in sc across row.
Row 7: 3ch, *MB, 3dc*, to last two sts, MB, 1dc, rep across row.
Rows 8–10: 1ch, work in sc across row.
Repeat rows 3–6 once more.
Fasten off.

fur stitch

This stitch is usually worked on the wrong side of the fabric. Using your left index finger and working in single crochet, you will create a lovely loopy effect on the right side.

HOW TO MAKE FUR STITCH

Insert the hook into the stitch on the previous row. Take the hook over the working yarn and hook it both behind and in front of the index finger. Pull the two loops of yarn through, releasing the long loop over the finger to lie at the back of the work. Take the yarn over the hook once more and pull it through to complete the stitch.

TRY THIS FUR STITCH PATTERN

Foundation chain: ch an even number of sts.
Foundation row: 1ch, sc across row.
Row 1: 1ch, sc every stitch creating a loop on each one.
Continue, repeating both these 2 rows.
Fasten off.

bullion stitch

Bullion stitches are made by wrapping the yarn several times around the hook. You can make quite demure ones by wrapping 7 times or bumper bullions wrapped 12 times.

HOW TO MAKE A BULLION STITCH

Wrap the yarn over the hook the appropriate number of times. Insert the hook into the stitch on the previous row, take the yarn over and pull it through. Take the yarn over again and pull the yarn through all the loops on the hook, easing them off one at a time.

TRY THIS BULLION STITCH PATTERN

Foundation chain: ch an even number of sts.
Foundation row: 3ch, dc across row.
Row 1: 3ch, work bullion (wrapping yarn 8 times around hook), * 1ch, miss 1, work bullion*. Rep to end.
Continue, repeating these 2 rows.
Fasten off.

sewing

There are a few different methods of sewing your crocheted fabrics, using either a tapestry needle or crochet hook. Each method gives a slightly different finish, although they work best when joining edges with the same number of stitches or rows.

WOVEN SEAM

This invisible seam provides a neat flat finish suitable for garments and fine fabrics.

Place the two pieces of crocheted fabric side by side, aligning the stitches and with the right sides down. Thread a tapestry needle with matching yarn. Insert the needle from right to left through the loops of the first stitch on the right-hand fabric and then through the loops of the first stitch on the left-hand fabric. Now insert the needle from left to right through the loops of the second stitch on the left-hand, and then the right-hand fabric. Gently pull the yarn through and the crocheted pieces together.

Continue to work up the seam, one pair of stitches at a time, in the same way. After every few stitches, gently pull the yarn and draw the pieces together. Don't pull the yarn up too tightly because the seam should stretch as much as the crocheted fabric. Sew the ends of yarn into the seam and trim neatly.

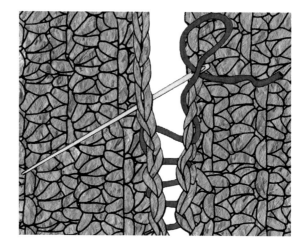

OVERCAST SEAM

This method is often used to join motifs together.

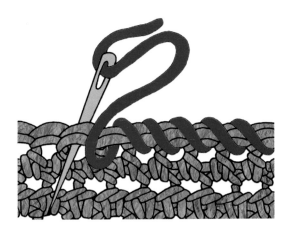

Place the two pieces of crocheted fabric side by side with the right side down. Insert the needle, threaded with matching yarn, at right angles through the back loops of a corresponding pair of stitches on each edge. Continue to overcast each pair of stitches together in the same way, gently pulling the yarn and the pieces together. When the seam is finished, sew the ends of yarn into it and trim them neatly.

SLIP STITCH SEAM

This method produces a firm seam, which is ideal for items such as bags that do not need to stretch much. You can work the seam on the wrong side, or on the right side to make a neat ridge.

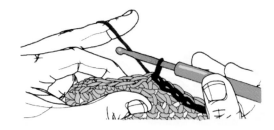

Hold the two pieces of crocheted fabric together, aligning the stitches. Insert the crochet hook under both loops at the top of a pair of corresponding edge stitches. Draw through the yarn with the hook to make a slip stitch. Continue in the same way to complete the seam. Fasten off and trim the yarn ends.

DOUBLE CROCHET SEAM

This seam will give you a decorative edging on the right side, although it is most often worked on the wrong side.

Work with a crochet hook in the same way as for a slip stitch seam, using single crochet instead of slip stitch.

shaping

Shaping crocheted fabric is really simple. There are a few different methods to try, but each one will provide you will a nice neat increase or decrease.

INCREASING INTO A STITCH

You may need to increase the number of stitches in order to widen the fabric at either or both ends of a row, to give it shape along a row or to keep the rounds in a circular shape flat. There is one basic method of doing this and it can be worked using any type of stitch.

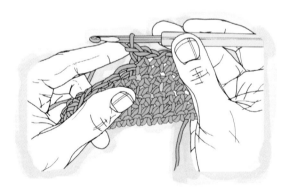

Simply work two or more stitches, depending on the pattern or the increase required, into one stitch on the previous row or round.

DECREASING A STITCH

There are two ways of decreasing stitches—both can be worked using any type of stitch. Different patterns may suggest one or the other method, and each produces slightly different results.

The simplest way to decrease a stitch is to miss out working into the next stitch on the previous row or round, working into the one after it instead. Depending on the pattern or how many stitches you need to decrease, you can miss out one or more stitches along a row. ➤

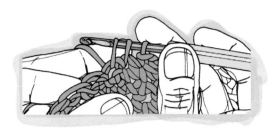

Alternatively, you can decrease a stitch by working two stitches together. For example with single crochet, draw the yarn through the next stitch on the previous row or round, but don't complete the stitch. You should now have two loops on your hook. Now insert the hook into the next stitch on the previous row or round and draw the yarn through to give three loops on the hook.

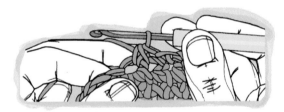

Take the yarn over the hook again and pull it through all three loops.

You can use this method to decrease more than one stitch by working into more stitches on the previous row or round and pulling the yarn through all the extra loops on the hook in one action.

beads & sequins

Adding beads or sequins is an easy way to give crochet a really glamorous look and it's so easy to do! Choose beads or sequins with holes big enough to take the crochet yarn.

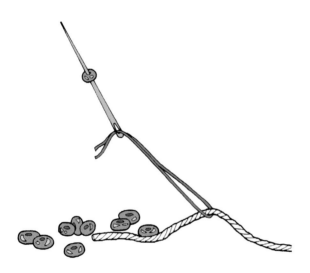

① Select a sewing needle that will go through the holes in the beads or sequins. Take a length of sewing thread and thread the two ends through the needle. Thread the end of the crochet yarn through the loop made by the sewing thread.

② Thread the beads or sequins onto the needle, over the sewing thread and onto the crochet yarn. The pattern will tell you how many to thread on, but always add a few more—you can always take them off the other end of the yarn later. Push the beads or sequins along to give you enough yarn to make the required length of foundation chain. ➤

3 When you want to add a bead or sequin into the crochet, first insert the hook into the stitch below. Before you complete the new stitch, simply push one bead or sequin up the yarn to sit next to the crochet hook.

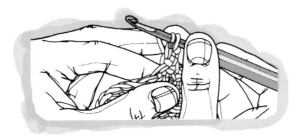

4 Draw the yarn through with the bead or sequin, making sure that it sits neatly at the front of the work.

5 Keeping the bead securely in place, complete the stitch. Repeat as necessary according to the pattern.

RACHEL'S & SARAH'S TIP: When working with beads, always make sure you have threaded the right amount onto the yarn before starting a project and, at the beginning of a row, always check you have enough to work to the end as it can be very frustrating to run out halfway through. The threading on part can be a long process but it's always worth it in the long run as it saves time doing it again.

You could also try threading on buttons and weaving them into your crocheted fabric—anything with a small hole will work. And, if you want something particularly decorative, try weaving in three or more beads or sequins at a time.

pom-poms & spirals

These are great to make when adding decoration to an accessory or customizing crocheted garments.

pom-poms

A great way to practice your shaping techniques. When you work a simple bobble, you will be working in a round to begin with and increasing and decreasing your stitches to form a bobble-like shape.

TRY THIS POM-POM PATTERN

Make 2ch, 8sc in second ch from hook, [2sc into next sc, 1sc into next sc] 4 times; [2sc into next sc, 1sc into each of next 2sc] 4 times; work 32 sc; [miss 1sc, 1sc into each of next 3sc] 4 times; [miss 1sc, 1sc into each of next 2sc] 4 times. Fasten off leaving a long end. Stuff the pom-pom with scraps of yarn and then close the hole.

The 3 pom-pom samples above were crocheted in DK yarn with a 4.5mm hook.

spirals

If you use a bulky yarn, this spiral will make a funky scarf or a trim for a sweater. The more stitches you increase by and the more rows you add, the more effective the twist spiral becomes.

TRY THIS SPIRAL PATTERN

Foundation chain: ch any number of sts, depending on how long you want the spiral to be.
Foundation row: 1ch, sc 2 or 3 times into each st. Repeat foundation row as desired.

The 3 spiral samples above were crocheted in bulky yarn with a big hook.

felted crochet

Felting is such fun to do and is used in some of the brilliant projects in this book. You just need to choose a yarn with 70 percent or more pure wool and an open stitch to help the fibers bind together.

FELTING IN A WASHING MACHINE

Set the washing machine to a 60°F wash. Put your crocheted fabric in the machine with some washing detergent and an old towel or other old items to balance the load.

It may take more than one wash to achieve the effect you want, or you could try hand-felting to agitate the fabric more.

FELTING BY HAND

Put on a pair of rubber gloves. Run first hot and then cold water over the fabric, agitating it with your hands and rubbing in a dash of detergent. Alternate the hot and cold water treatment until you have achieved the amount of felting you want.

Once the crocheted fabric is felted, leave it to dry away from direct sunlight. When it is completely dry, you can cut it into shapes.

See page 80 for our pattern for felted oven mitts

abbreviations

It won't take long for you to get used to the abbreviations used in crochet. Once you familiarize yourself with these, you'll start to see through the jargon.

ABBREVIATIONS

bsc	Beaded single crochet
ch	Chain
ch sp	Chain space
dc	Double crochet
dec	Decrease
htr	Half treble
hdc	Half double crochet
inc	Increase
MB	Make a bobble stitch
Rep	Repeat
RS	Right side
sc	Single crochet
SP	Work 1sc into next sc 2 rows below
ss	Slip stitch
sts	Stitches
tr	Treble
tog	Together
WS	Wrong side
yo	Yarn over
yrh	Yarn round hook

TERMS

Group: Several stitches worked into the same place/stitch.

Yarn over: Wrap the yarn from the ball over the hook in order to make a new loop. This is always done in an counter-clockwise direction.

Base chain: The length of chains you make at the very start of your project (your width).

Turning/Starting chain: The amount of chains you make at the beginning of a row. (This will depend on the type of stitch you are working with.)

Asterisks and parentheses: You will find these a lot in patterns when there is a need to repeat certain rows or rounds. You will often repeat what is within the asterisks/parentheses.

accessories for guys & girls

Once you've come to grips with your hook and yarn, try some of the fun accessories in this chapter. I've designed these projects to let you experiment with different stitches and techniques. Whether it's the bracelets, the winter scarf, or perhaps the bobble purse, after completing just a few of these projects you will soon have the confidence to create your own designs…enjoy!

Rachel x

girl's winter scarf

Using really bulky yarn and a big hook makes your crochet grow fast. The fat yarn and hook make this a great design for practicing your crochet technique, plus it's easy to do and you can never have enough scarves!

MATERIALS Super chunky thickness 100% merino yarn, 3 x 100g balls in different shades (A), (B), and (C).

HOOK 15mm

GAUGE 6 stitches to 4in/10cm and 4 rows to 6in/15cm over pattern.

PATTERN

Using A, make 7ch.

Foundation row: 1sc into 2nd ch from hook, 1sc into each ch. 6sc.
Row 1: 2ch [miss 1sc, 1dc into next sc, 1dc into missed sc] 3 times.
Row 2: 1ch, 1sc into each dc.
Row 3: As row 1.
Row 4: As row 2. Change to B.
Row 5: 1ch, 1sc into each sc.

Rep rows 1–5, using each color in turn, until you have your required length of scarf, ending with row 4. Fasten off.

bobble purse

My roommate is forever saying I need a purse for all the yarn and equipment strewn around our apartment, so I came up with this gorgeous solution. Of course, it's not only great to keep your crochet stuff in order, it's big and sturdy enough to tote around as a purse.

MATERIALS

Super chunky thickness 100% merino yarn, 2 x 100g balls. Bulky yarn in contrasting color for attaching handles.
1 x pair of straight bamboo or wooden handles.

HOOK

12mm

GAUGE

6 stitches and 6½ rows to 4in/10cm square over single crochet.

ABBREVIATION

MB: Work 4 complete dc into same stitch (i.e., leaving last loop of each dc on hook), yarn round hook and pull through all 5 loops to make 1 st.

PATTERN

Back
Make 18ch.
Foundation row (WS): 1sc into 2nd ch from hook, 1sc into each ch. 17sc.
Rows 1 and 2: 1ch, 1sc into each sc.
Row 3: 1ch, 2sc, MB, 5sc, MB, 5sc, MB, 2sc.
Rows 4 and 5: 1ch, sc2tog, sc to end. 15sc.
Row 6: 1ch, 1sc into each sc.
Row 7: 1ch, 4sc, MB, 5sc, MB, 4sc.
Rows 8 and 9: 1ch, sc2tog, sc to end. 13sc.
Row 10: 1ch, 1sc into each sc.
Row 11: 1ch, 1sc, MB, 4sc, MB, 4sc, MB, 1sc.
Rows 12 and 13: 1ch, sc2tog, sc to end. 11sc.
Rows 14 and 15: 1ch, 1sc into each sc.
Fasten off. Work front to match.

Sides

Make 6ch.

Foundation row (WS): 1sc into 2nd ch from hook, 1sc into each ch. 5sc.

Rows 1 and 2: 1ch, 1sc into each sc.

Row 3: 1ch, 2sc, MB, 2sc.

Row 4: 1ch, 1sc into each sc.

Repeat rows 1–4, 9 times.

Work rows 1 and 2 again.

Fasten off.

FINISHING

With the wrong sides together, pin, then baste the sides in place. Using a smaller crochet hook, join with a row of single crochet through both thicknesses.

Using a smaller crochet hook and the bulky yarn (something that matches your purse), attach the handles by working single crochet into each st across the top of purse and under and over the handle.

Once complete, line the purse with a piece of sturdy fabric.

THINGS TO DO WITH YOUR CROCHET HOOK:

#1 MAKE POPSICLES

soft sequined scarf

Who said crochet isn't glamorous? Make this elegant scarf and glam it up with loads of sparkly sequins.

MATERIALS   Mohair and silk 4 ply mix yarn, 2 x 25g balls in different shades. Assorted sequins.

HOOK   4.5 mm

GAUGE   Small circle 3in/7.5cm diameter. Large circle 5in/13cm diameter.

PATTERN

Small circle (make 12)
Use shade A double.

Make 4ch, ss into first ch to form a ring.
Round 1: 3ch, 2dc into ring, 3ch [3dc into ring, 3ch] 4 times, ss into top of 3ch.
Round 2: Ss into each of 2dc, ss into ch sp, 3ch, 2dc into same sp as ss, 3ch [3dc into next ch sp, 3ch] 4 times, ss into top of 3ch.
Fasten off.

Large Circle (make 7)
Use shade B double.

Make 4ch, ss into first ch to form a ring.
Round 1: 3ch, 2dc into ring, 3ch, [3dc into ring, 3ch] 4 times, ss into top of 3ch.
Round 2: Ss into each of the 2dc, ss into ch sp, [3ch, 2dc, 3ch, 3dc, 3ch] all into same sp as ss, [3dc, 3ch] twice into each ch sp, ss into top of 3ch.
Round 3: Ss into each of 2dc, ss into ch sp, 3ch, 2dc into same as ss, 1ch, *[3dc, 1ch] twice into next ch sp, [3dc, 1ch] into next ch sp; rep from * 3 times, [3dc, 1ch] twice into last ch sp, ss into top of 3ch.
Round 4: Ss into each of 2dc, ss into ch sp, 3ch, 2dc into same sp as ss, 1ch, [3dc, 1ch] into each ch sp, ss into top of 3ch. Fasten off.

FINISHING

Sew a pair of small circles between each large circle, as shown. Sew some sequins in the center of each circle.

beaded bracelet

Making jewelry with beads and yarn is not nearly as tricky as you might expect. It's really quite easy, and there are loads of creative possibilities by combining colors, textures, and beads.

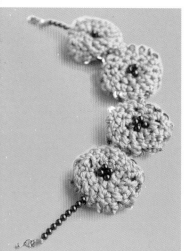

MATERIALS 100% cotton yarn (in between 4 ply and double knitting thickness),
1 x 50g ball. Beads or sequins.
Clasp fasteners.
Small piece of felt.

HOOK 3.5mm

PATTERN

Bobbles (make 4)
Thread 64 beads or sequins onto yarn.
3ch, ss into first ch to form a ring.
Round 1 (WS): 1ch, 8sc into ring, ss into first sc.
Round 2: 1ch, 2sc into each sc, ss into first sc. 16sc.

Rounds 3 and 4: 1ch, [slide 1 bead up and work 1sc into next sc] to end, ss in first sc.
Round 5: 1ch, [1sc into next sc, miss next sc] to end. 8sc.
Round 6: As round 5. 4sc.
Fasten off.

FINISHING

Sew up the bobbles, push through the beads or sequins, and flatten.
Sew a sprinkling of beads in the center of each bobble.
Cut 4 felt circles and sew one to the back of each bobble.
Cut a 16in/40cm length of yarn. Attach one half of the fastener securely to the end of yarn, thread on 6–10 beads followed by the 4 bobbles, another 6–10 beads then the other half of the fastener.
Fasten off securely.

wire necklace & earrings

You can also use crocheting techniques to make jewelry from beads and wire. This project uses basic techniques, plus it's a great way to create some cheap but funky jewelry pieces.

MATERIALS   Colored wire.
1 pack of beads.
Necklace fastener.
2 earring hooks.

HOOK   4.5mm

PATTERN

Necklace
Circle with beaded edge (make 4):
Make 5ch.
Foundation row: 1sc into 2nd ch from hook, 1sc into each ch. 4sc.
Row 1: 1ch, 1sc into each sc.
Rows 2–15: As row 1.
Fasten off.

Squash to form a small circle. Using a length of wire join 18–20 beads around the edge of the circle, weaving the wire in and out of the circle to secure.

Wire beaded circle (make 3):
Thread 25 beads on the working wire.
Make 6ch.
Foundation row: Push bead up to last ch, 1sc into 2nd ch from hook, [push bead up to last sc, 1sc into next ch] to end. 5sc.
Row 1: 1ch, [push bead up, 1sc into next sc] to end.
Rows 2–4: As row 1.
Fasten off. Mold each wire piece into a circular shape.

End piece (make 2):
Thread 14 beads on working wire.
Make 3ch.
Foundation row: Push bead up to last ch, 1sc in 2nd ch from hook, push bead up to last sc, 1sc in next ch. 2sc.
Row 1: 1ch [push bead up, 1sc in next sc] twice.
Rows 2–6: As row 1.
Fasten off.

Earrings
Make 2 circles with beaded edge, as given for necklace.

FINISHING

For the necklace, secure one half of the fastener onto a length of wire, then weave the wire in and out through one end piece, [across one small circle with beaded edge then across one wire beaded circle] 3 times, across the last small circle with beaded edge, then other end piece. Adjust the length of wire to fit your neck, then secure the other end of fastener in place.

For the earrings, using a small length of wire attach the earring hooks to small circles.

THINGS TO DO WITH YARN:

#1 TIE YOUR HAIR BACK WITH IT

jewelry bags

These beautiful, delicate little bags are ideal for jewelry, makeup or as a very special gift bag for your mom or a close buddy.

MATERIALS   Mohair and silk 4 ply mix yarn,
1 x 25g ball. I used 1 x 25g ball each
in blue and soft purple
20in x 1/8in wide ribbon.

HOOK   5mm

GAUGE   11 stitches and 8 rows to 4in/10cm
square.

ABBREVIATION

MB: Work 3 incomplete dc into same st (i.e. leaving last loop of each dc on hook), yarn round hook and pull through all 4 loops to make 1 st.

PATTERN

Main part
Using yarn double, make 30ch.
Foundation row: 1sc into 2nd ch from hook,
1sc into each ch. 29sc.

Row 1: 1ch, 1sc into each sc.
Row 2 (RS): 3ch, 1dc into next sc,
[MB, 1dc into each of next 2sc] to end.
Rep rows 1 and 2, 5 times, then work row 1 again.
Next row: 4ch, miss first sc, 1tr into each sc. Work 3 rows sc.
Fasten off.

Base
Make 4ch, ss into first ch to form a ring.
Round 1: 3ch, 7dc into ring, ss into top of 3ch.
Round 2: 3ch, 1dc into same place as ss, 2dc into each dc, ss into top of 3ch.
Round 3: 1ch, 2sc into each st, ss into first sc.
Fasten off.

FINISHING

Join the row ends of the main part. With WS together, sew the base to the main part. Weave the ribbon in and out of dtr row on the main part and tie in a bow.

guy's tie

This was an idea I came up with for my friend's band—stripey ties that they could wear at their gigs. Using denim yarn gives this design a modern twist and works day and night.

MATERIALS 100% cotton denim double knitting yarn. I used bright blue (A) and navy blue (B).

HOOK 4.5 mm

GAUGE 12 stitches and 12 rows to 4in/10cm square over single crochet, using yarn double.

PATTERN

Use yarn double. With A, make 8ch.
Foundation row: 1sc into 2nd ch from hook, 1sc into each ch. 7sc.
Dc row: 1ch, 1sc into each sc.
Work in sc for 14½in occasionally changing color to make a stripey fabric.
Next row: 1ch, sc2tog, sc to end of row.
Next row: 1ch, sc2tog, sc to end of row. 5sc.
Work a further 35½in sc.
Fasten off.

FINISHING

You will need to line the finished tie with thick fabric to stop it from twisting and to give it firm support. Don't forget, denim yarn decreases in size when washed!

hat & glove set

Cheer yourself up over the winter months with this adorable hat and glove set. Who wouldn't want to brave the short days looking this cute?

MATERIALS Chunky thickness 100% merino yarn, 2 x 50g balls in different shades. I used purple (A) and rose (B).

HOOK 9mm

GAUGE 8 stitches to 4in/10cm.

PATTERN

Hat

Using A, make 6ch, ss into first ch to form a ring.
Round 1: 3ch, 9dc into ring, ss into top of 3ch.
Round 2: 3ch, working into back loop only work 1dc into same place as ss, 2dc into each dc, ss into top of 3ch. 20sts.
Round 3: As round 2. 40sts.
Rounds 4 and 5: 1ch, working into both loops work 1sc into each st, ss into first sc.
Round 6: Change to B. 1ch, 1sc around stem of each sc, ss into first sc.

Round 7: As round 4.
Round 8: Change to A. Work as round 6.
Round 9: As round 4.
Rounds 10 and 11: As rounds 6 and 7.
Round 12: Change to A, 1ch, 1sc into top of each sc, ss into first sc.
Round 13: 1ch, *miss first sc, sc into next 2sc* Rep to end, miss last st, ss into first sc.
Fasten off.

Flower

Using A, make 5ch, ss into first ch to form a ring.
Round 1 (WS): 1ch, 7sc into ring, ss into first sc.
Round 2: [5ch, ss into next sc] 7 times.
Fasten off.
For center make 4ch using B, ss into first ch to form a ring.
Round 1 (RS): 1ch, 5sc into ring, ss into first sc.
Fasten off. Sew in the center of flower. Sew the flower onto the side of hat.

Gloves

Using A, make 17ch.

Foundation row (RS): 1sc into 2nd ch from hook, 1sc into each ch. 16sc.

Row 1: 1ch, 1sc into each sc.

Row 2: Change to B, 1ch, 1sc around stem of each sc.

Row 3: 1ch, 1sc in top of each sc.

Rows 4 and 5: Change to A. Work as rows 2 and 3.

Rows 6 and 7: Change to B. Work as rows 2 and 3.

Rows 8 and 9: Change to A. 1ch, 1sc into top of each sc.

Row 10: 3ch, miss first sc, 1dc into back loop of each sc.

Row 11: Change to B, 3ch, miss first dc, 1dc into back loop of each dc, 1dc into top of 3ch.
Fasten off.

Flower (make 2)

Using A, make 3ch, ss into first ch to form a ring.

Round 1 (WS): 1ch, 5sc into ring, ss into first sc.

Round 2: [3ch, ss into next sc] 5 times.
Fasten off.

For center make 3ch using B, ss into first ch to form a ring.

Round 1: 1ch, 4sc into ring, ss into first sc.
Fasten off.

Join the seam of each glove and use a space between the stitches on the tenth row for the thumb hole. Sew the center onto the middle of each flower, then sew a flower onto the back of each glove.

THINGS TO DO WITH YOUR CROCHET HOOK:

#2 STIR YOUR TEA WITH IT

geometric scarf

My boyfriend wanted a scarf with a difference, so I came up with this contemporary design. Of course, it would be great for a girl as well. It's simply made up of double squares crocheted together, so you can make it as long as you like by adding more squares. Easy!

MATERIALS Super chunky thickness 100% merino yarn, 3 x 100g balls in different shades. I used dark brown (A), chocolate brown (B), and sand (C).

HOOK 12mm

GAUGE 6 stitches and 7 rows to 4in/10cm square over single crochet.

PATTERN

Using A, make 11ch.
Foundation row: 1sc into 2nd ch from hook, 1sc into each ch. 10sc.
Rows 1–3: Using A, 1ch, 1sc into each sc.
Rows 4–7: Using B, 1ch, 1sc into each sc.
Rows 8–11: Using C, 1ch, 1sc into each sc.
Fasten off.

Make 9 more squares.

FINISHING

Place the squares in whatever order you like, horizontal or vertical, alternating them to create your own design. Sew up using the woven seam method (see page 37).

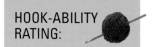

sling bag

Great for a guy or a girl. This bag has a contemporary, utilitarian design, and is big enough to fit your work books and newspapers.

MATERIALS
Super chunky thickness 100% merino yarn, 3 x 100g balls in one shade (A) and 2 x 100g balls in another (B).

HOOK
15mm

GAUGE
5½ stitches and 6½ rows to 4in/10cm square over single crochet.

PATTERN

Back
Using A, make 2ch.
Foundation row: 3sc into 2nd ch from hook.
Begin increase pattern.
Row 1: 1ch, 2sc into first sc, 1sc into next sc, 2sc into last sc. 5sc.
Rows 2–4: 1ch, 2sc into first sc, 1sc into each sc to last sc, 2sc into last sc. 11sc.
Row 5: 1ch, 1sc into each sc.
Rep rows 2–5 once. 17sc.
Break off A.
Join in B, rep rows 2–5 once. 23sc.

Break off B.
Join in A.
Begin decrease pattern.
Next 10 rows: 1ch, miss first sc, 1sc into each sc to last 2sc, miss 1sc, 1sc into last sc. 3sc.
Fasten off.

Front
Work as back.

Strap and gusset
The strap and gusset for this bag are crocheted all in one.
Using B, make 5ch.
Foundation row: 1sc in 2nd ch from hook, 1sc in each of next 3ch. 4sc.
Next row: 1ch, 1sc in each sc.
Continue until strip fits around 3 sides and is long enough to go over shoulder. Fasten off.

FINISHING

Join the ends of the strap and gusset and sew to 3 sides of the front and back using the woven seam method, leaving the remainder for the shoulder strap.

crocheting
for an occasion

By now, you've probably noticed that a whole world of crochet opportunities has opened up. I've designed these projects with both fun and function in mind. They will give you the confidence to experiment with a fabulous range of yarns and develop techniques including beading, felting, color-work and even creating your own works of art.

Sarah

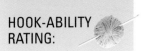

place mat & coasters

These are practical AND stylish. If you're a tableware afficionado, match the colors to your china for the ultimate in dinner party style. If you're not, choose colors that will go with everything and keep your precious tabletops protected!

MATERIALS

Linen double knitting yarn, 1 x 50g ball, used double throughout (A).
Aran thickness 100% bamboo yarn, 1 x 50g ball (B).
100% cotton 4 ply yarn, 1 x 50g ball. Used double throughout (C).

HOOKS

4mm and 5mm

GAUGE

13 stitches and 10 rows to 4in/10cm over hdc.

PATTERN

Place mat
Using 5mm hook and A, make 27ch.
Foundation row: 1hdc into second ch from hook, 1hdc into each ch.
Row 1: 1ch, 1hdc into each hdc.
Rep row 1 until you have made a square.
Fasten off.
With RS facing and using C, work a sc edging around square, working extra stitches into the corners, ss into first sc. Work 1 round in B and then C. Fasten off.

Large motifs
Make 1 each in A, B and C.
Round 1: Using 4mm hook, make 4ch, work 13dc into fourth ch from hook, ss into top ch. 14 sts.

Round 2: 3ch, 1dc into same place as ss, [1dc into next dc, 2dc into next dc] 6 times, 1dc into next dc, ss into top of 3ch.
Fasten off.

Small
Make 1 each in A and C.
Using 4mm hook work Round 1 as large motif.
Fasten off.

FINISHING

Press. Using the photograph on page 76 as a guide, sew the motifs to the mat.

Coaster
Using 5mm hook and A, make 12ch.
Work as place mat on 11hdc.

Motifs
Work 1 large motif each in A and C, but begin round 2 with 1ch, then work sc instead of dc.
Work 1 small motif in B.

FINISHING

As for place mats.

THINGS TO DO WITH YARN: #2 TIE YOUR ASPARAGUS

felted oven mitts

These oven mitts will ensure you remain safe yet stylish in even the most heated of situations. Be warned though, they're not suitable for use in or around a naked flame, but they are great for handling hot pots and pans. This design allows you to try a new technique: felting.

MATERIALS Chunky thickness 100% merino yarn, 4 x 50g balls (A).
Super chunky thickness 100% merino yarn, 1 x 50g ball (B).

HOOK 8mm

GAUGE Don't worry too much about gauge, as this will alter when the mitts are felted.

PATTERN

Main strip
Using A, make 16ch.
Foundation row: 1sc into 2nd ch from hook, 1sc into each ch. 15sc.
Row 1: 1ch, 1sc into back of loop of each sc.
Continue in pattern as set in Row 1 and at the same time inc 1 st at each end of next and following alternate rows until there are 23 sts.*
Work a further 68 rows in pattern.
Dec 1 st at each end of next row and following alternate rows until 15 sts remain.
Work 2 rows. Fasten off.

Pads (make 2)
Using A, work as main strip to *.
Work a further 14 rows.
Fasten off.

FINISHING

With the RSs together, sew the pads to the corresponding position of the main strip using backstitch. Turn right side out.

Place in an old pillowcase and wash at 140°F along with a couple of towels to balance the load (see page 44).

Once felted, pull into shape and allow to dry flat. When completely dry, use a large knitter's needle and yarn B to embellish with blanket stitch. Secure first stitch at one edge of the oven mitt and then work from left to right. Insert the needle close to the edge, bring back out over the thread loop and pull taut. Continue working evenly spaced stitches in this way along the edge of the oven mitt, taking care to only work through one layer of each mitt.

coffee press cover & mug warmers

I came up with this cute design to keep my coffee piping hot and make hot mugs easy to handle. When your friends visit for coffee they'll love the individual style.

MATERIALS Cotton blended Double knitting yarn, 3 x 50g ball in different shades (A), (B), and (C).
Rowan buttons: 3 x 00354, 4 x 00380.

HOOK 5mm

GAUGE 17 stitches and 22 rows to 4in /10cm over sc.

ABBREVIATIONS

SP: Work 1sc into next sc 2 rows below.

PATTERN

Coffee press cover
Using A, make 49ch.
Foundation row (RS): 1sc into 2nd ch from hook, 1sc into each ch. 48sc.
Row 1: 1ch, 1sc into each sc.
Rows 2–3: as row 1, changing to B during last sc of row 3.
Row 4: 1ch, [3sc, 2SP]; to last 3sc, 1sc into each sc.
Row 5: As row 1, changing to A during last sc.
Rows 6–7: As row 1, changing to C during last sc of row 7.
Row 8: 1ch, 2sc, [2SP, 3sc] to last sc, 1sc in last sc.
Row 9: As row 1, changing to A during last sc.
Rows 10–11: As row 1, changing to B at end of row 11.
Row 12: 1ch, 1sc, [2SP, 3sc], to last 2sc, 2SP.
Row 13: As row 1, changing to A during last sc.
Rows 14–25: As row 1, changing to B at end of row 25.
Rows 26–27: As rows 4–5.
Rows 28–29: As row 1. Fasten off.

Button band

With RS facing and C, work 25sc evenly along the left edge. Work 6 rows sc. Fasten off.

Buttonhole band

With RS facing and C, work 25sc evenly along right edge.

Work 3 rows sc.

Buttonhole row: 1ch, 1sc into next 3sc, [3ch, miss next 3sc, 1sc into next 5sc] twice, 3ch, miss next 3sc. 1sc into last 3sc.

Next row: 1ch, 1sc into each sc and 3sc into each ch sp. Work 2 rows sc. Fasten off.

Using B, work 1ss around stem of each sc of last row. Fasten off.

Press. Sew on larger buttons.

Mug warmer (make 2)

Using B, make 39ch.

Work as coffee press cover to end of row 3, changing to A during last sc of row 3.

Row 4: As for coffee press cover.

Row 5: As row 1, changing to B during last sc.

Rows 6–9: As row 1.

Fasten off.

Buttonhole band

With RS facing and C, work 9sc evenly along left edge.

Work 3 rows sc.

Buttonhole row: 1ch, 1sc into next 2sc, 1ch, miss 1sc, 3sc, 1ch, miss 1sc, 1sc into last 2sc.

Next row: 1ch, 1sc into each sc and ch sp.

Work 1 row sc. Fasten off.

Using A, work 1ss around stem of each sc of last row. Fasten off.

Press. Sew on smaller buttons.

THINGS TO DO WITH YOUR
CROCHET HOOK:
USE IT AS A BOOKMARK

#3

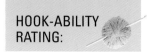

beaded pencil case

Inspired by all the wonderful stationery on the market, this pencil case is glamorous, yet practical. The combination of beading worked into a closely woven fabric means that none of your vital accessories can escape.

MATERIALS   100% cotton double knitting yarn,
1 x 50g (A).
Small amount of Slick (B).
78 x size 6 beads. I used SB2630
(orange/lime).
60 x size 6 beads. I used SB209
(pink/clear).

HOOK   3mm

GAUGE   19sc and 22 rows to 4in/10cm.

PATTERN

Thread beads onto yarn alternating 13 orange and 12 pink, until all beads are threaded.

Using A, make 34ch.
Foundation row: 1sc into 2nd ch from hook, 1sc into each ch. 33sc.
Row 1: 1ch, 1sc into each sc.
Row 2: As row 1

Row 3 (WS): 1ch, 1sc into each of next 4sc, [slide bead up and work 1sc into next sc, 1sc into next sc, 1sc into next sc] 13 times, 1sc into each of last 3sc.
Rows 4–6: As row 1.
Row 7: 1ch, 1sc into each of next 5sc, [slide bead up and work 1sc into next sc, 1sc into next sc] 12 times, 1sc into each of the last 4sc.
Rows 8–10: As row 1.
Rep rows 3–10, 4 times, then work rows 3–6 again.
Fasten off.

FINISHING

Do not press.
With RS facing and using B, work 1ss around the stem of each sc of last row. Fasten off.
Using the photograph as a guide, fold the fabric to form an "envelope." With RS facing and using B, join sides by working a row of sc through all thicknesses.
Fasten off.

artwork

The idea behind this artwork is to encourage you to appreciate how far crochet has traveled from its original image. The instructions should be seen as a springboard for you to develop your own ideas. Have fun!

square of circles

MATERIALS Small amounts of 100% cotton yarn (in between 4 ply and double knitting thickness).
Rowan buttons: I used 4 x 00378, 3 x 00347, 2 x 00349.
Canvas block 6in x 6in/15cm x 15cm (available from discount art stores).
Double-sided tape.
1/3in x 1in/9mm x 25mm brass curtain rings.

HOOK 3.5mm

PATTERN

Small circle (make 4)
Use color combinations of your choice.
Round 1: Work 30sc into curtain ring. Join with a ss. Change color.
Round 2: 1ch, 1sc into each sc. Join with a ss.*
Fasten off.

Large circle (make 5)
Use color combinations of your choice.
Work as small circle to*. Change color.
Round 3: 1ch, 1sc into same place, [1sc into next sc, 2sc into next sc], to last sc, 1sc into last sc. Join with a ss. Fasten off.

FINISHING

Press circles.
Attach strips of double-sided tape to the canvas and then arrange the circles according to your taste.
Place the button in the center of each circle.

wire flowers

MATERIALS Hand-made paper (or background of choice), measuring 1¹/₈in larger than chosen canvas block. Canvas block as before. Selection of beads. 0.200mm silver plated craft wire, colored craft wire. I used opaque purple.

HOOK 3.5mm

PATTERN

Large flower
Use silver wire double throughout.
Make 5ch, ss in first ch to form a ring.
Round 1: 3ch, 25dc into ring, ss into top of 3ch.
Round 2: 1ch, [3ch, miss next dc, 1sc into next dc] to end, 3ch, ss into first ch. Fasten off.

Medium flower
Make 1 with a single thread of silver wire and one with silver wire used triple throughout.
Make 5ch, ss into first ch to form a ring.
Round 1: 1ch, 15sc into ring, ss into first ch.
Round 2: 1ch, [3ch, miss next sc, 1sc into next sc] to last sc, 3ch, ss into first ch. Fasten off.

Small flower
Make 1 with a single thread of silver wire. Work as medium flower to end of round 1. Fasten off.

Make another in the same way, with a single thread of silver wire and a single thread of opaque purple. For the top layer of this flower, use a single thread of opaque purple and work as medium flower to end of round 1. Fasten off.

FINISHING

Position the flowers on the paper and thread the loose wires through to the back. This will help secure them. Stitch the beads into the flowers and through the paper to accent different parts of the flowers. Attach the paper to the canvas to the block using double-sided tape and miter the corners to achieve a neat edge.

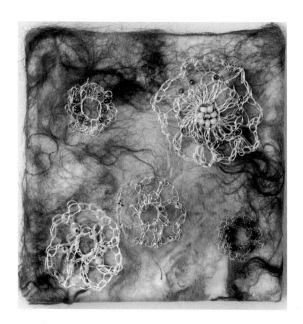

THINGS TO DO
WITH YARN:

#3

HANG TEALIGHTS

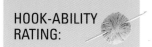

pillow cover

Here, I've woven a basic mesh with fabrics to achieve a net-like texture. Adding fabrics and fibers of your choice will enable you to match it to your own surroundings.

MATERIALS

Cotton blended Double knitting yarn, 1 x 50g ball.
12in/30cm of Kaffe Fassett† Fabric Collection in Roman Glass, cut into 1in/2.5cm strips. I used red and green.
Pillow form, 12in/30cm square.

HOOK

5mm

GAUGE

17 stitches to 4in/10cm.

PATTERN

Front
Make 54ch.
Foundation row: 1dc into 6th chain from the hook, [1ch, miss 1ch, 1dc into next ch] to end.
Row 1: 4ch, miss first dc [1dc into next dc, 1ch] to end, 1dc in 2nd of each ch.
Rep row 1 until front is square.
Fasten off.

FINISHING

Press.
Fold fabric strips in half, (so that pattern is showing) and weave in and out of the mesh as illustrated or according to a pattern of your choice. Tucking in any loose ends as you go, slip stitch the panel onto your pillow form. Back with a contrasting fabric or make another panel to match or contrast.

greeting cards

Individually designed cards are a great way to tell someone you really care about them. You could also get creative and make invitations or thank-you cards.

jolly jacquard (far left)

MATERIALS Small amount of 100% cotton yarn
(in between 4 ply and double knitting
thickness). I used a beige (A),
chocolate brown (B), bronze (C), and
butter yellow (D).
1 blank card, approx 6in/15cm square.
Double-sided tape.

HOOK 3.5mm

PATTERN

Note—Work last sc before changing color in this way: insert hook into st, yarn round hook and draw loop through, now change color and draw new color through 2 loops on hook. Strand color not in use loosely across WS of panel.

Crochet panel
Using A, make 16ch.
Foundation row (RS): Using A, 1sc into 2nd ch from hook, 1sc into each of next 2ch [using B, 1sc into each of next 3ch; using A, 1sc into each of next 3ch] twice.

Row 1: Using A, 1ch, 3sc, [3dc in B, 3sc in A] twice.
Row 2 and 3: As row 1.
Rows 4–7: Using C, 1ch, 3sc [3sc in D, 3sc in C] twice.
Rows 8–11: As row 1.
Rep rows 4–11 once.
Fasten off.
Using D, work 1 round of sc evenly around panel, work 2sc into each corner, ss in first sc. Fasten off.

FINISHING

Press.
Attach 3 strips of double-sided tape to blank card and add crocheted panel.

flower garden (far right, page 94)

Use a background paper as inspiration for your crocheted greeting. Look out for papers with interesting shapes and color schemes and let inspiration take over.

MATERIALS Odds and ends of 100% cotton yarn (in between 4 ply and double knitting thickness). I used an orange (A) and purple (B), silver (C), and claret (D). Card blank approx 4¾in/12cm square. Double-sided tape.

HOOK 3.5mm

PATTERN

First circle (from left)
Using A, make 6ch, ss into first ch to form a ring.
Round 1: 3ch, 19dc into the ring, ss into top of 3ch.
Round 2: Fasten off A; join D. 1sc into each dc, ss into first sc. Fasten off.

Second circle
As first circle, using B and C.

Third circle
As first circle, using C and A.

Fourth circle
Using A, make 6ch, ss into first ch to form a ring.
Round 1: 1ch, 10sc into ring, ss into first sc. Fasten off A; join B.
Round 2: 3ch, 1dc into same place as ss, 2dc into each sc, ss into top of 3ch. Fasten off.

FINISHING

Press.
Cut the background paper to size and attach to the card with double-sided tape.
Run a strip of double-sided tape where the background paper meets the card.
Attach the motifs so that they overlap slightly and form an interesting line.

THINGS TO DO WITH YOUR CROCHET HOOK:

#4 STIR YOUR COCKTAIL

hot-water bag cover

This design challenges the rather frumpy image of a hot-water bag cover! Now you can keep snug without compromising your street cred.

MATERIALS

Cotton blended Double knitting yarn: 1 x 50g (A), small amounts of (B) and (C).

HOOK

5mm

GAUGE

14 htr and 10 rows to 4in/10 cm.

ABBREVIATIONS

Hdc2tog: leaving last loop of each st on hook work 1hdc into each of next 2 sts, yrh and pull through all 3 loops.

PATTERN

Hot-water bag cover
Using A, make 29ch.
Foundation row: 1sc into 2nd ch from hook, 1sc into each ch. 28sc.
Row 1: 2ch, 1hdc into each sc.
Row 2: 2ch, 1hdc into each hdc.
Rows 3–7: As row 2, changing to B during last st of row 7.
Row 8: 1ch, 1sc into each hdc changing to C during last st of row.

Row 9: 1ch, 1sc into each sc, changing to A during last st of row.
Row 10: 2ch, 1hdc into each sc.
Row 11: 2ch, hdc2tog, 1hdc into each hdc to last 2 sts, hdc2tog.
Rows 12–13: As row 11. 22 sts.
Row 14: As row 2. Mark each end of last row with a contrast thread.
Row 15: As row 2.
Row 16: 2ch, 2hdc into next hdc, 1hdc into each hdc to last st, 2hdc into last st.
Rows 17–18: As row 16. 28 sts.
Rows 19–33: As row 2.
Row 34: 2ch, [hdc2tog] twice, 1hdc into each hdc to last 4 sts, [hdc2tog] twice.
Row 35: As row 34.
Row 36: 2ch, [hdc2tog] 3 times, 1hdc into each hdc to last 6 sts, [hdc2tog] 3 times. 14 sts.
Rows 37–39: As row 2, changing to B during last st of row 39.
Row 40: 1ch, 1sc into each hdc, changing to C during last st.
Row 41: 1ch, 1sc into each sc, changing to A during last st of row.
Row 42: As row 1.
Row 43: As row 16. 16 sts.
Rows 44–45: As row 2. Mark each end of last row with a contrast thread.

Rows 46–47: As row 2.
Row 48: As row 11. 14 sts.
Row 49: As row 2, changing to C during last st.
Row 50: As row 40 and changing to B during last st.
Row 51: As row 41 and changing to A during last st.
Row 52: As row 1.
Rows 53–54: As row 2.
Row 55: 2ch, 2hdc into each of next 3hdc, 1hdc into each hdc to last 3hdc, 2hdc into each hdc. 20 sts.
Rows 56–57: 2ch, 2hdc into each of next 2hdc, 1htdc into each hdc to last 2hdc, 2hdc into each hdc. 28 sts.
Rows 58–64: As row 2.
Fasten off.

Large motif
Using A, make 5ch.
Round 1: 1ch, 12sc into ring, ss into first sc. Change to B.
Round 2: 3ch, 1dc into same place as ss, 2dc into each sc, ss into top of 3ch. 24 sts. Change to C.
Round 3: 3ch, 1dc into same place as ss, [1dc into next dc, 2dc into next dc] to last dc, 1dc in last dc, ss into top of 3ch. 36 sts.
Fasten off.

Medium motif
Using B in place of A, and A in place of B, work as large motif to end of round 2. Change to C.
Round 3: 1ch, 2sc into same place as ss, [1sc into next dc, 2sc in next dc] to last dc, 1sc in last dc. 36 sts.
Fasten off.

Small motif
Using C, make 5ch, ss into first ch to form a ring.
Round 1: 3ch, 19dc into ring, ss into top of 3ch. Change to B.
Round 2: 1ch, 1sc into each dc. Fasten off.

FINISHING

Using the photograph as a guide, fold the work along the top of the marked rows, matching up shaping to form an "envelope."
With RS of work facing and using C, work a row of sc through both layers at the sides and top, taking the shaping around the top of the bag into account (3 layers of work will need to be joined where the flap is formed).

Slip stitch motifs into place, again using the photograph as a guide.

handy bottle bag

We all know how important it is to carry water with us, especially on hot days. Now you can keep your hands free and avoid bulging purses with this fun and practical bottle carrier.

MATERIALS

100% cotton denim double knitting yarn, 1 x 50g ball (A) and (B).

HOOK

4mm

GAUGE

19 stitches and 22 rows to 4in/10cm measured over sc.

PATTERN

Bottle carrier:
Using A, make 4ch.
Round 1: 11dc into fourth ch from hook, ss into top ch. 12 sts.
Round 2: 3ch, 1dc into same place as ss, 2dc into each dc, ss into top of 3ch. 24 sts.
Round 3: As round 2. 48 sts.
Round 4: 1ch, 1sc into same place as ss, 1sc into each dc, ss into first dc.
Round 5: 1ch, 1sc into each sc, ss into first sc.
Rounds 6 and 7: As round 5.
Rounds 8 and 9: Using B, as round 5.
Rounds 10–12: using A, as round 5.
Round 13: 1ch, 1sc into same place as ss, 3ch, miss 3sc [1sc into next sc, 3ch, miss 3sc] to end, ss into first sc.

Round 14: 1ch, 1sc into same place as ss, 3ch, [1sc into sc, 3ch] to end, ss into first sc.
Rounds15–30: As round 14.
Round 31: 1ch, 1sc into each sc and 3sc into each ch sp, ss into first sc. 48 sts.
Work 4 rounds sc in A, 2 rounds in B and 3 rounds in A.
Fasten off.

Strap

Using A, make a 55in/140cm length of ch.
Foundation row (WS): 1hdc into 3rd ch from hook, 1hdc into each ch.
Edging (RS): With RS of foundation row facing and using B, work 1sc into each st of last row, then 1sc into each of foundation ch. Fasten off.

FINISHING

Press.
Find the midpoint of the strap and slip stitch into place across the base of carrier. Thread each remaining length through the bars at opposite sides of the mesh and slip stitch into place up the sides of the carrier until you reach the top. Place one strap end underneath the other in order to achieve the desired length and slip stitch into place.

THINGS TO DO WITH YARN:
#4 TIE A BUNCH OF FLOWERS

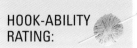

rag rug

Inspired by the idea of making rugs from rags, this version uses a luxury silk/
cotton yarn while retaining a sense of simplicity. This rug would look great in a
bathroom or at the entrance to your beach hut! My tension is only a guide; it
really doesn't matter if your rug is bigger or smaller.

MATERIALS Cotton blended Aran thickness yarn:
2 x 50g hanks in four shades. I used
white, lime, green and blue.
Buttons (optional).

HOOK 8mm

The rug is worked in three panels, joined and
trimmed with single crochet and decorated with
shell buttons.

GAUGE 9sc and 10 rows to 4in, using
yarn double.

PATTERN

Panel 1

Use yarn double throughout.
Using lime, make 19ch.
Foundation row (WS): 1sc into 2nd ch from hook,
1sc into each ch. 18sc.
Row 1: 1ch, 1sc into each sc.
Continue in sc stripes: 1 row green •
3 rows blue • 1 row white • 1 row lime
1 row blue • 3 rows green • 3 rows white
1 row lime • 2 rows green • 2 rows blue
1 row white • 4 rows green • 1 row lime
1 row blue • 5 rows green • 1 row blue
3 rows white • 1 row lime • 2 rows blue
2 rows green • 1 row lime • 1 row blue
1 row white. Fasten off.

Panel 2

Use yarn double throughout. Using blue, make
19ch. Work as Panel 1 but using the following stripe
sequence:
3 rows blue • 3 rows lime • 1 row white
2 rows blue • 2 rows green • 1 row lime
4 rows blue • 1 row white • 1 row green
5 rows blue • 1 row green • 3 rows lime

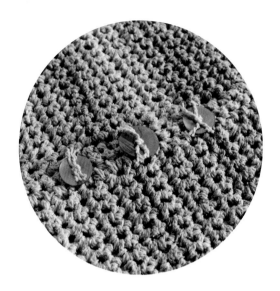

1 row white • 2 rows green • 2 rows blue
1 row white • 1 row green • 1 row lime
2 rows white • 1 row blue • 3 rows green
1 row lime • 1 row white • 1 row green
Fasten off.

Panel 3

Use yarn double throughout. Using lime, make
19ch. Work as Panel 1 but using the following stripe
sequence:
4 rows lime • 1 row blue • 1 row green
5 rows lime • 1 row green • 3 rows white
1 row blue • 2 rows green • 2 rows lime
1 row blue • 1 row green • 1 row white
2 rows blue • 1 row lime • 3 rows green
1 row white • 1 row blue • 1 row green
3 rows lime • 3 rows green • 1 row blue
2 rows lime • 2 rows green • 1 row white
Fasten off.

FINISHING

Press. Use yarn double throughout. With RS
facing and using white, work 2 rows sc along the
row ends of left-hand edge of panel 2. With RSs
together and using white, join panel 3 to the edging
of panel 2 working a row of sc through both panels.
Fasten off.

With RS facing and using white, work 2 rows sc
along the row ends of right-hand edge of panel 1.
Join the edging of panel 1 to the lower edges of
panels 2 and 3. Fasten off.

With RS facing and using white, work 1 round sc
around the outer edge, working 3sc into each
corner, ss into first sc. Fasten off.

Using the photograph as a guide, sew on the
buttons by pulling the yarns through to the front
of the buttons and tying off to secure.

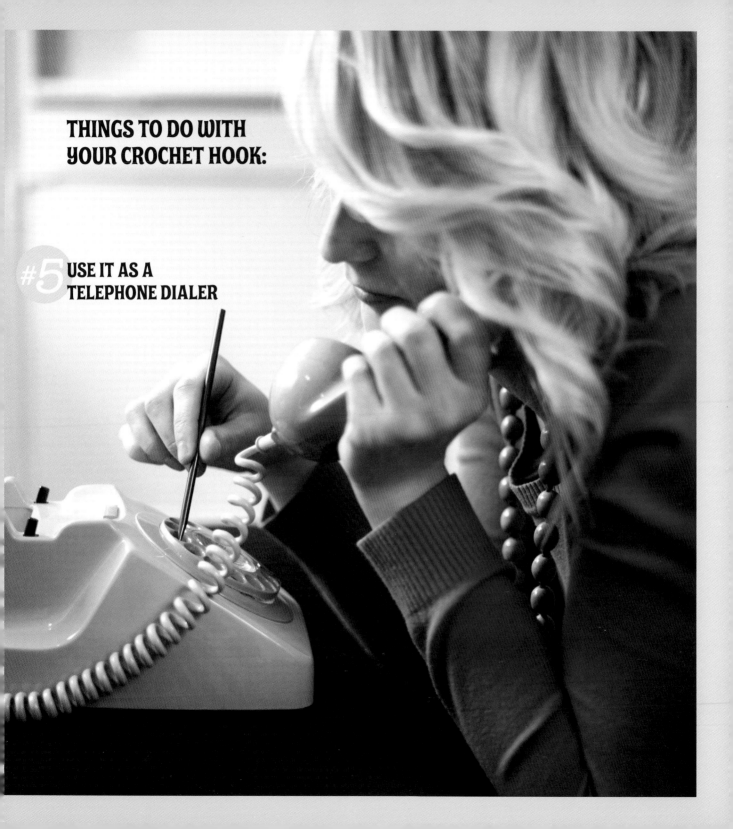

**THINGS TO DO WITH
YOUR CROCHET HOOK:**

#5 **USE IT AS A
TELEPHONE DIALER**

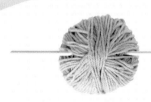

customizing designs

Recently there seems to be huge interest in recycling and customizing clothes. I regularly take scissors to my latest charity buy or old, tired denims and plain tops. Customizing is a fast and cost-effective method of making something new and fashionable. Visit your local thrift shop or rummage through your drawers for things that are crying out for a revamp. All you need is a bit of confidence and some creative thinking.

Rachel x

edgings

My edging designs are straightforward and will take no time at all to crochet up. By adding a simple trimming to a garment or accessory you can easily transform something plain into something very decorative. And don't hesitate to experiment with yarn shades.

edging 1

MATERIALS Chunky thickness 100% merino yarn, 1 x 50g ball.

HOOK 9mm

PATTERN
Make a multiple of 3ch plus 1 extra.
Row 1: 1sc into 2nd ch from hook, 1sc into each ch.
Row 2: [1ss into sc, 5dc into next sc, 1ss into next sc] to end. Fasten off.

edging 2

MATERIALS Mohair and silk 4 ply mix yarn, 1 x 25g ball (A), 1 x 25g ball (B).

HOOK 4.5mm

PATTERN
Use yarn double throughout.
Using A, make length of ch required for edging.
Row 1: 1sc into 2nd ch from hook, 1sc into each ch.
Row 2: 3ch, miss first sc, 1dc into each sc.
Row 3: 1ch, 1sc into each dc, 1sc into top of 3ch.
Rows 4–5: As rows 2–3.
Row 5: Join B to first sc, 1ss in first sc, [10ch, 1ss in next sc] to end. Fasten off.

edging 3

MATERIALS   Aran thickness lambs wool and mohair mix yarn, 1 x 50g ball.

HOOK   5mm

PATTERN

Thread on your buttons—the number will depend on the length of edging required.
Make a multiple of 7ch plus 4 extra.
Row 1: 1sc into 2nd ch from hook, 1sc into each ch.
Rows 2 and 3: 1ch, 1sc into each sc.
Row 4: 1ch, 1sc into first sc, [wrap yarn 8 times around hook, insert hook in next st, slide button up to hook, take yarn over hook at left of button and complete sc then pull hook through all 8 loops, 1sc into each of next 6sc] to end, ending 1sc into last sc. Fasten off.

edging 4

MATERIALS   Linen double knitting yarn, 1 x 50g ball.

HOOK   4.5mm

PATTERN

Make a multiple of 5ch plus 2 extra.
Row 1: 1sc into 2nd ch from hook, 1sc into each ch.
Row 2: 1ch, 1sc into each sc.
Row 3: 1ss into first sc, [5ch, miss 4sc, 1ss into next sc] to end.
Row 4: 1ch, 7sc into each ch sp.
Fasten off.

edging 5

MATERIALS   Aran thickness 100% bamboo yarn, 1 x 50g ball.

HOOK   4.5mm

PATTERN

Thread beads onto yarn before beginning; the number will depend on length of edging required.
Make a multiple of 3ch, plus 1 extra.
Rows 1: 1sc into 2nd ch from hook, 1sc into each ch.
Row 2: 1ch, 1sc into each sc.
Row 3: [1ss into sc, 2ch, push bead up to last ch, 2ch, miss 1sc, 1ss into next sc] to end. Fasten off.

girl's casual top

This is a great way to reinvent your clothes when you're a bit short of money. Visit your local thrift shop, pick out a pretty top, have a rummage in your yarn collection for something pretty to match and customize your fabric with a delicate crocheted edging. This is so easy to do and a great way to recycle and use up your odds and ends of yarn.

MATERIALS Pure silk double knitting yarn,
1 x 50g ball.

HOOK 3.5mm

PATTERN

Edging
Make a length of ch to fit around lower edge of top, working a multiple of 3ch plus 1 extra.
Work in sc for as many rows as you like. For my border I worked 6 rows in sc before working my lace trim.

Lace trim
Row 1: [Ss into sc, 5ch, ss into 3rd ch from hook (picot), 2ch, miss 1sc, ss into next sc] to last 3 sts, ss into next st, 5ch, ss into 3rd ch from hook, miss next sc, 1dc into last sc.
Row 2: Ss into first picot, [5ch, ss into next picot] to end. Fasten off.

Inset
Make 5ch
Foundation row: 1sc into 2nd chain from hook, 1sc into each ch. 4dc
Row 1: 1ch, 2sc into first sc, 1sc into each sc.
Rep row 1 until inset is required size and there is a multiple of 3sc.
Work 2 rows of lace trim as edging. Fasten off.

FINISHING

To sew on your edging, first pin the edging around the lower edge of the top and using a fine needle and matching sewing thread, sew loosely in place. Sew inset in place.

denim skirt

Everyone loves their denim, but they do tend to look the same. Try adding your own touches to some old denim pieces or high-street basics with this stylish edging.

MATERIALS 100% cotton denim double knitting yarn, 2 x 50g balls.

HOOK 5mm

PATTERN

Edging
Foundation ch: Make a length of ch to fit around hem of skirt, working a multiple of 4 sts plus 2 extra.
Foundation row (RS): 1sc into 2nd ch from hook, 1sc into each ch.
Row 1: 1ch, 1sc into each sc.
Row 2: 1ch, 1sc into first sc, [8ch, miss 3sc, 1sc into next sc] to end.
Row 3: [5sc, 3dc 3tr] into each ch sp.

Belt
Make 5ch, ss first ch to form a ring.
Foundation row: 4ch, [4dc, 3ch, 5dc] into ring, turn.
Row 1: 4ch, [4dc, 3ch, 4dc] into 3 ch sp, ss into top of turning chain, turn.
Rep row 1 for required length for belt.

FINISHING

Sew the edging along the bottom of skirt with matching thread. Weave the belt under the belt loops on the skirt and tie.

girl's bow top

If your summer vacation is looming but your clothes funds are running low, then why not try customizing one of your plain tank tops or t-shirts? This is a really feminine way of adding detail to a plain top.

MATERIALS
100% cotton double knitting yarn, 2 x 50g balls.

HOOK
4.5mm

PATTERN

Bow
Bullion stitch: Wrap yarn 8 times around hook, insert hook into next st, yrh and pull loop through then, one at a time, pull through each of the 8 strands of yarn.
Make 13ch.
Foundation row: 1sc into 2nd ch from hook, 1sc into each ch. 12sc.
Rows 1 and 2: 1ch, 1sc into each sc.
Row 3 (RS): 3ch, miss first sc, [1 bullion st into next sc, 1ch, miss 1sc] 5 times, 1dc into last sc.
Rows 4–6: 1ch, 1sc into each st.
Rep rows 3–6, 15 times.
Fasten off.

Knot
Make 7ch.
Foundation row: 1sc into 2nd ch from hook, 1sc into each ch. 6sc.
Row 1: 1ch, 1sc into each sc.
Rep row 1, 16 times.
Fasten off.

Belt
Make 7ch.
Foundation row: 1sc into 2nd ch from hook, 1sc into each ch. 6sc.
Row 1: 1ch, 1sc into each sc.
Rep row 1 until belt fits around tank top at waistline.
Fasten off.

FINISHING

Fold the main fabric to form a bow shape. Wrap the middle around the center of bow and sew securely in place. Join the ends of the belt. Attach the bow to the belt, then sew the belt onto the tank top using matching sewing thread.

recycled purse

This is so easy to do; all you need is an old sweater, some yarn, and a pair of scissors and, voila, your sweater is now a purse!

MATERIALS Aran thickness lambs wool and mohair mix yarn, 2 x 50g balls in different shades (A) and (B). Snap.

HOOK 5mm

DIRECTIONS FOR CUSTOMIZING

1. Pull out a sweater you don't wear any more, or find a second-hand one from a thrift shop (make sure it is at least 70 percent wool).

2. First felt the sweater by putting it in the washing machine at 140°F (see page 44). Once dry, cut off the top part and the sleeves.

3. You should now have two rectangular pieces. Mine are 22¹/₂in x 10¹/₄in /32cm x 26cm.

4. Cut up the sleeves to use as the sides and base of the purse, pin all the pieces together and sew up inside out using a matching color of sewing thread.

ABBREVIATIONS

MB: Work 6 incomplete dc into same st until you have 7 loops, pull yarn through all 7 loops to make 1 st.

PATTERN

Handles (make 2)
Using A, make 8ch.
Foundation row: 1sc into 2nd ch from hook, 1sc into each ch. 7sc.
Row 1: 1ch, 1sc into each sc.
Row 2: As row 1.
Row 3: 1ch, 1sc into each of 3sc, MB into next st, 1sc into each of 3sc.
Rows 4–6: 1ch, 1sc into each st.

Rep rows 3–6, 11 more times (or more until you have achieved your required length).

Small pom-pom (make 2)

Using B, make 2ch, 8sc in 2nd ch from hook, [2sc into next sc, 1sc into next sc] 4 times; [2sc into next sc, 1sc into each of next 2sc] 4 times*; work 32 sc; ** [miss 1sc, 1sc into each of next 3sc] 4 times; [miss 1sc, 1sc into each of next 2sc] 4 times. Fasten off leaving a long end. Stuff the pom-pom with scraps of yarn and then close the hole.

Large pom-pom (make 1)

Using A, work as small pom-pom to * [2sc into next sc, 1sc into each of next 3sc] 4 times; work 40sc; [miss 1sc into each of next 4sc] 4 times. Complete as small pom-pom from **.

FINISHING

With WSs together, join the handles, stuff with yarn and sew inside the top of purse at each side. Sew the snap inside the top of the purse. For the drawstring, use 1 strand A and 1 strand B together. Starting at the center front, thread the yarn in and out through the purse at the base of the rib. Attach the pom-poms to the ends of the drawstring.

THINGS TO DO WITH YARN:

#5 STRING UP YOUR VEG

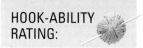

girl's elegant top

By adding this simple neckline to a thrift shop purchase you can give a plain-looking garment a completely different style. Once felted, it only takes a couple of hours to make.

MATERIALS Mohair and silk 4 ply mix yarn (A), 1 x 25g ball.
Aran thickness lambs wool and mohair mix yarn, 2 x 50g balls (B).
35$\frac{1}{2}$in/90cm of $\frac{1}{2}$in/15mm wide satin ribbon.

HOOK 4.5mm

DIRECTIONS FOR CUSTOMIZING

Find a long-sleeved, over-sized sweater in a thrift shop or use an existing one (make sure it is at least 70 percent wool).

Felt it by putting it in the washing machine at 140°F (see page 44). Cut the sleeves and neck off.

Pattern for neckline

Using mohair and silk together make a length of ch to fit around neck.

Row 1 (RS): 1sc into 2nd ch from hook, 1sc into each ch.

Row 2: 1ch, 1sc around stem of each sc.

Rep these 2 rows for the required depth of neckline. Now begin to decrease.

Next row: 1ch, [miss 1sc, 1sc into each of next 2sc] to end.

Next row: 1ch, 1sc around stem of each sc.

Next row: 1ch, [miss 1sc, 1sc into each of next 2sc] to end. Fasten off.

FINISHING

Join ends using slip stitch method (see page 21) and sew around the neck. Thread ribbon through the top edge, pull tight to pull neckline together and tie in a bow.

index

standard yarn weight system

Categories of yarn, gauge ranges, and recommended needle and hook sizes

* GUIDELINES ONLY: The chart below reflects the most commonly used gauges and needle or hook sizes for specific yarn categories.

** Lace weight yarns are usually knitted or crocheted on larger needles and hooks to create lacy, openwork patterns. Accordingly, a gauge range is difficult to determine. Always follow the gauge stated in your pattern.

*** Steel crochet hooks are sized differently from regular hooks— the higher the number, the smaller the hook, which is the reverse of regular hook sizing.

Source: Craft Yarn Council of America's www.YarnStandards.com

Yarn Weight Symbol & Category Names	0 LACE	1 SUPER FINE	2 FINE	3 LIGHT	4 MEDIUM	5 BULKY	6 SUPER BULKY
Type of Yarns in Category	Fingering 10-count crochet thread	Sock, Fingering, Baby	Sport, Baby	DK, Light Worsted	Worsted, Afghan, Aran	Chunky, Craft, Rug	Bulky, Roving
Knit Gauge Range* in Stockinette Stitch to 4 inches	33–40** sts	27–32 sts	23–26 sts	21–24 sts	16–20 sts	12–15 sts	6–11 sts
Recommended Needle in Metric Size Range	1.5–2.25 mm	2.25–3.25 mm	3.25–3.75 mm	3.75–4.5 mm	4.5–5.5 mm	5.5–8 mm	8 mm and larger
Recommended Needle U.S. Size Range	000–1	1 to 3	3 to 5	5 to 7	7 to 9	9 to 11	11 and larger
Crochet Gauge* Ranges in Single Crochet to 4 inch	32–42 double crochets**	21–32 sts	16–20 sts	12–17 sts	11–14 sts	8–11 sts	5–9 sts
Recommended Hook in Metric Size Range	Steel*** 1.6–1.4 mm	2.25–3.5 mm	3.5–4.5 mm	4.5–5.5 mm	5.5–6.5 mm	6.5–9 mm	9 mm and larger
Recommended Hook U.S. Size Range	Steel*** 6, 7, 8 Regular hook B–1	B–1 to E–4	E–4 to 7	7 to I–9	I–9 to K–10 1/2	K–10 1/2 to M–13	M–13 and larger